P9-DTN-251

The New GLASS House

The New GLASS House

JAMES GRAYSON TRULOVE

Bulfinch Press
New York · Boston

Copyright © 2006 by Grayson Publishing

All rights reserved. No part of this book may be reproduced in any form or
by any electronic or mechanical means, including information storage and
retrieval systems, without permission in writing from the publisher, except
by a reviewer who may quote brief passages in a review.

Bulfinch Press

Time Warner Book Group
1271 Avenue of the Americas, New York, NY 10020
Visit our Web site at www.bulfinchpress.com

First Edition: May 2006

Trulove, James Grayson.
    The new glass house / James Grayson Trulove. — 1st ed.
        p. cm.
    ISBN 0-8212-6202-5
1. Glass construction — United States. 2. Architect-designed houses —
United States. 3. Architecture — United States — 20th century.
4. Architecture — United States — 21st century. 1. Title.
NA7208.T78 2006
728'.37 — dc22   2005022161

Title page: Packard Komoriya residence;
photograph by Hoachlander-Davis Photography

PRINTED IN CHINA

Contents

INTRODUCTION

LIGHT, REFLECTION, TRANSPARENCY

About ten years ago I had the opportunity to visit the iconic Glass House in New Canaan, Connecticut, designed by Philip Johnson as his own residence. Although completed in 1949, the steel and glass structure, sitting like a large display case on a perfectly manicured carpet of grass, seemed timeless, ephemeral. Although its livability may be questioned—but for the brick cylinder enclosing the bathroom, there is no privacy—its subsequent influence on architects cannot be underestimated. So as I began to consider houses for inclusion in *The New Glass House,* I recalled much that I admired about the Glass House—the fantastic light, the reflective surfaces, the great views, the transparency—while being mindful of the need to identify houses that are fundamentally livable and representative of a range of housing types and styles. Thus, among the fourteen projects chosen for this book are town houses, primary and secondary homes both large and modest in size, as well as a personal library. None of the houses chosen are all-glass structures, but they all count glass as a significant material in their design and construction, from windows and doors to walls, floors, guardrails, and stair treads.

Dramatic uses of glass can be found in the Cliffside House by Wood+Zapata Architects and the Gulf Coast Residence by Toshiko Mori. In the former, vast expanses of green-tinted glass walls open the house to views of an active but distant volcano. The green, reflective glass causes the 8,000-square-foot house, sited on a steep, heavily treed lot, to disappear into the landscape when viewed from a distance. Architect Mori chose blue-tinted glass for her modernist structure on the Gulf of Mexico. Spanning floor to ceiling and wall to wall, the glass casts a pale glow within the interior. Inside, glass floors and a large central atrium with a glass prism allow light to flow to the ground level.

Transparency and framing are the themes of the Sagaponac House by Hariri & Hariri. Large, deeply set rectangles of glass provide a frame for the flat landscape of eastern Long Island. When viewed from the outside, they frame the interior of the house. Their alignment is such that from some exterior vantage points, the house becomes a lens through which to see the landscape beyond.

In a dense urban area, town houses whose facades are primarily glass can also act as display cases allowing a passerby to examine often intimate details of the occupants' lives, as in the case of the Chicago Town House. Architect Alexander Gorlin has designed an all-glass town house for a bachelor where even the closets are open to inspection from the street.

Finally, for the Scholar's Library, architect Peter Gluck designed a completely glass-enclosed study that sits atop ten thousand books. From this high perch, the occupant enjoys solitude among the trees.

The Glass House inspired me. I hope these and the other projects in *The New Glass House* will inspire readers to use glass to open up their own homes or those they are designing.

A glass prism within the atrium of the Gulf Coast
Residence diffuses daylight into a spectrum of colors.
Photograph by Paul Warchol

CHICAGO TOWN HOUSE

ON DISPLAY

This town house for a bachelor in the Bucktown section of Chicago is a gleaming modern structure that floats above the more traditional homes in the neighborhood. The house is set back from the street behind a brick-walled garden. A steel-and-stone stairway cuts through the volume of the house, leading directly from the garden to the main living level on the second floor and to the third level and roof terraces above. On the main level, a double-height space contains the open loft of the kitchen, living, and dining areas. The vertically oriented living room is framed by large expanses of glass, which open onto the garden below and provide views of the street. A luminous screen of parachute-cloth curtains defines the space of the dining room, with its own terrace above the garage. On the lower level are a guest bedroom and an exercise space.

Above, a suspended glass box contains the master bedroom and bathroom. The glass shower and freestanding tub open directly onto the master bedroom. At both ends of this bathing-sleeping combination, glass walls afford views of the city. At the bedroom end, the view is through the open clothes closet, where the client's perfectly coordinated suits hang for all the world to see.

Materials are limited to a minimally cool palette of white-painted steel, white statuary marble for all counters, gray-toned stone floors from China, and white plaster walls.

ARCHITECT
Alexander Gorlin Architects
PHOTOGRAPHER
Michael Moran

ROOF DECK　　　THIRD-FLOOR PLAN　　　SECOND-FLOOR PLAN　　　FIRST-FLOOR PLAN

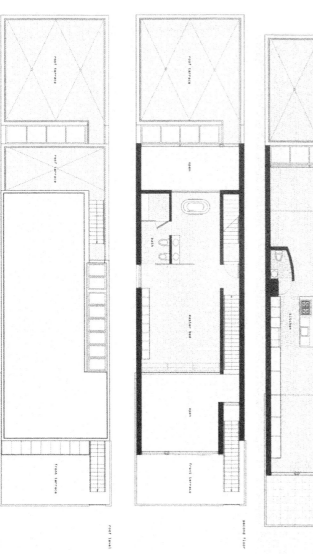

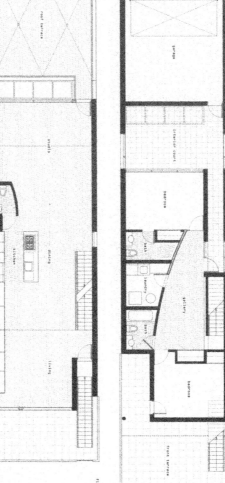

On the previous two pages, a two-story glass facade opens the house and its contents to the street. Within, parachute cloth is used for privacy on this level. Below, the living room is suspended above the garage, and entry is via stone steps leading from the front garden to the second-floor living area.

EAST ELEVATION

WEST ELEVATION

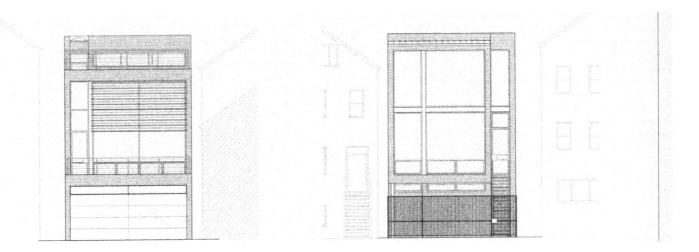

NORTH ELEVATION

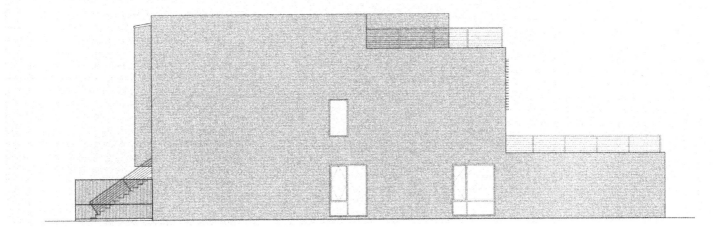

SOUTH ELEVATION

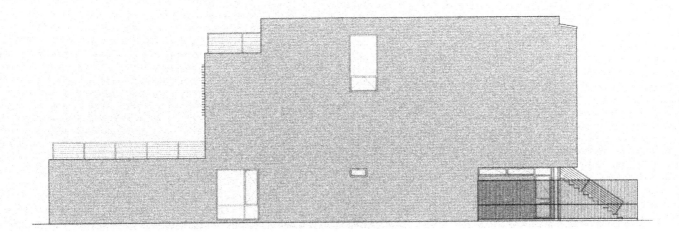

The main floor is loftlike, with an open living, kitchen, and dining area ideal for entertaining. The muted color palette consists of light gray stone floors, white plaster walls, and white marble countertops in the kitchen.

The master bedroom and bath are suspended above the living room. Privacy from the street is casually achieved by garment racks that utilize the owner's wardrobe as a curtain. A glass skylight above the stairs floods the interior with natural light.

The glass-enclosed shower, along with the rest of the master bathroom, opens directly onto the master bedroom.

Although this home has extensive glazing to take advantage of the tremendous views from its bluff-side perch, the stone and green-stained cedar exterior anchors it firmly into the rugged landscape.

SHELVING ROCK RESIDENCE

KEEPING A LOW PROFILE

Set on a bluff in a dense forest on the east shore of Lake George in New York, this vacation house will eventually serve as a full-time residence. The linear plan seeks to take advantage of the lake views, while the low roof profile and green-stained exterior cedar siding meld into the surrounding forest.

A substantial, solid facade greets visitors as they approach from the northeast along a winding lane that cuts through the forest. In contrast, the south face, which overlooks the lake, is almost entirely glazed and affords long views toward the lake and distant mountains. Thus, one passes through the opaque north entrance facade to discover the extraordinary setting of the house.

From the entry, one is drawn into the house by the extraordinary view through the Douglas fir screen and staircase of the Adirondack Mountains beyond. Forty-three hundred square feet of living space are linearly organized on two levels between the stairs and the glazed facade so that all major rooms have a view of the lake. The tandem living room, dining room, and kitchen flow easily into each other, creating a seamless living space. The relationship of these spaces is accentuated by a red-stained, plywood-paneled "tongue" that extends their combined length. To the northeast, a recessed stone-and-wood inglenook is an intimate counterpoint to the expansive views of the lake. Adjacent to the living room, the master bedroom opens onto a deck and has views through the forest to a secluded cove. The upper level accommodates two bedrooms and a recreation area.

ARCHITECT
Bohlin Cywinski Jackson
PHOTOGRAPHER
Nic Lehoux

SECOND-FLOOR PLAN

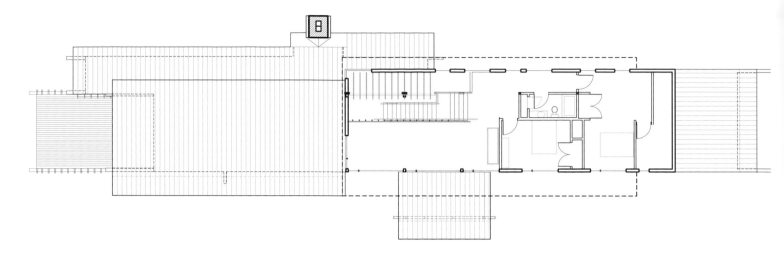

FIRST-FLOOR PLAN

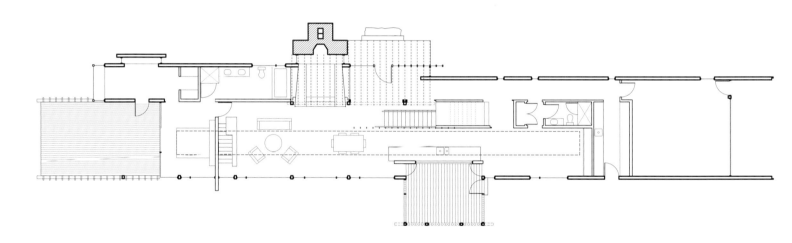

SITE PLAN

SECTION

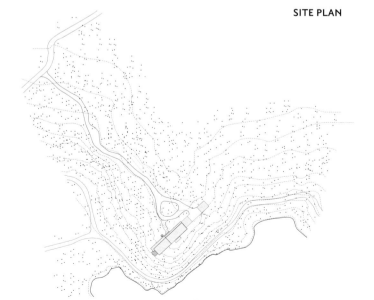

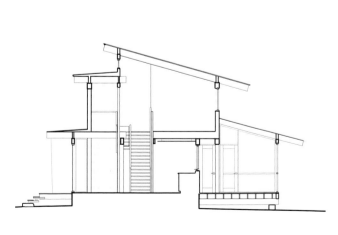

EAST ELEVATION

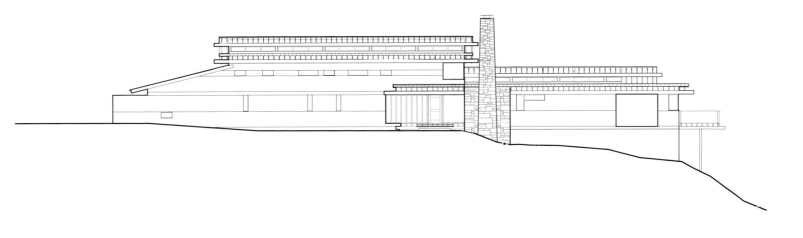

WEST ELEVATION

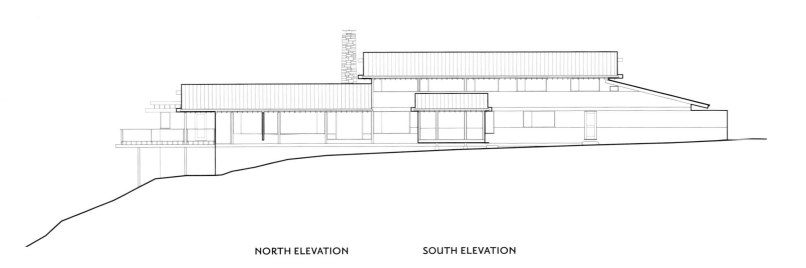

NORTH ELEVATION   ## SOUTH ELEVATION

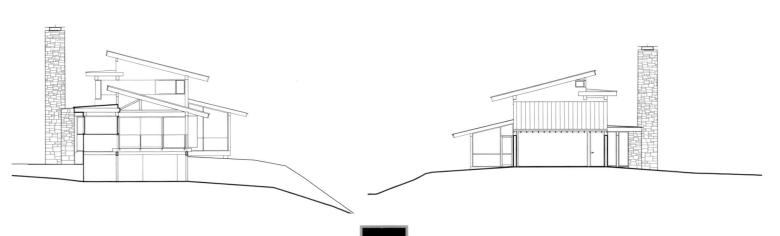

The house is barely visible when viewed from the lake. The long, low profile contributes to this camouflage. A tall stone chimney, which is part of an inglenook in the living room, is juxtaposed with the glazed entry to focus attention on the heart of the house.

The plan of the house is organized around the main staircase and an open-framework Douglas fir screen, which links the entry to the kitchen. Opposite the living room with its expansive glazing, the inglenook offers a cozy contrast.

The kitchen, dining area, and living area all flow seamlessly
one to the other along the glazed wall overlooking Lake
George. A red-stained plywood-paneled "tongue" extends
along the ceiling, visually linking these areas.

*The master bedroom is adjacent to the living area and is
encased in a glass box overlooking its own deck and
the forest.*

*From the entry, a visitor can see through the transparent
stairway, past the dining room to the view beyond.*

31

NGH

*This Galvalume and fiberboard dwelling is perched on a
steep slope above active railroad tracks, with dramatic views
of Puget Sound in the distance.*

MILEPOST 9

A TRAIN GOES THROUGH IT

Constructed above railroad tracks on a steep site in Seattle with water views extending into the distance, this house was built on the foundation of an existing house that was demolished. The house framing, while aggressive in its cantilevers and large openings, was designed to use as little steel as possible as a cost consideration.

The exterior materials were selected to be virtually maintenance free and cost-effective. The house consists of two boxes, one stacked atop the other. The upper volume is clad in a standard Galvalume sheathing, while the lower volume consists of cement fiberboard covered with an epoxy paint for maximum protection and durability.

The window system is a residential-grade thermal-break aluminum frame. The large window expanses were created by combining individual windows with an interior steel frame that also provides vertical structural support. The windows are installed within the openings of the steel frame, which is covered with matching anodized aluminum to create the appearance of a unified window system. From the interior the steel frame was left exposed, eliminating the need for trim around the windows.

ARCHITECT
E. Cobb Architects
PHOTOGRAPHER
Chris Eden

THIRD-FLOOR PLAN

MEZZANINE FLOOR PLAN

NORTH/SOUTH SECTION

SITE PLAN

EAST/WEST SECTION

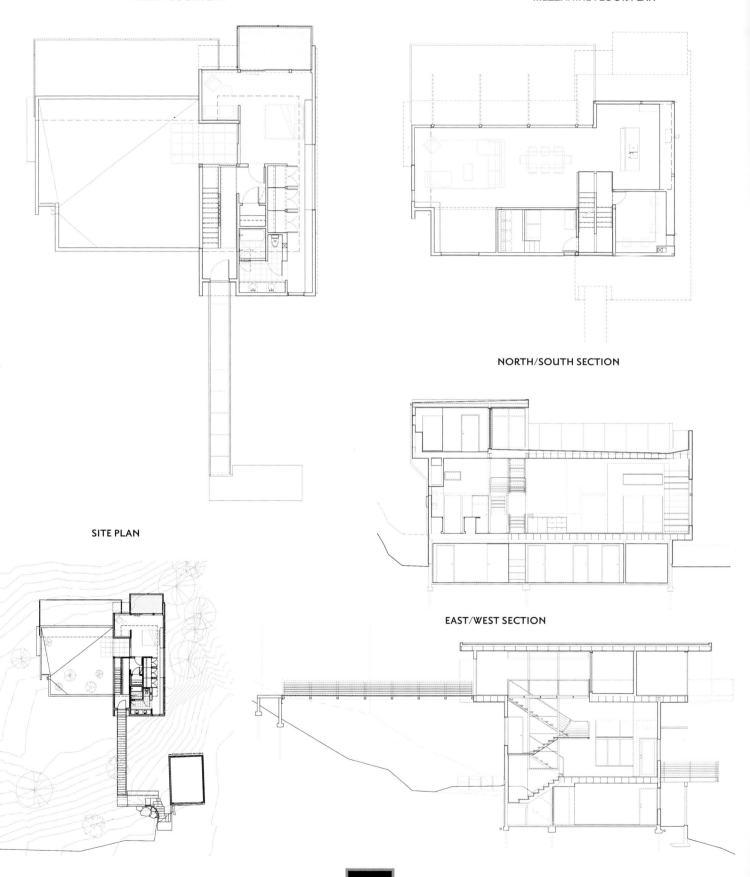

SECOND-FLOOR

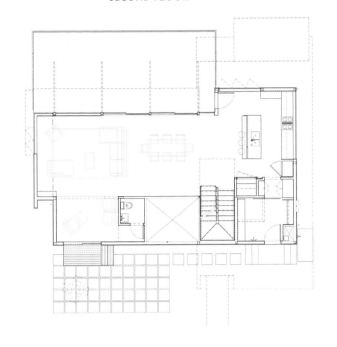

FIRST-FLOOR PLAN

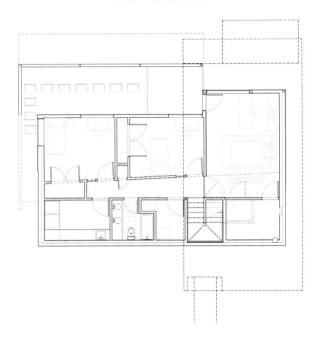

NORTH ELEVATION

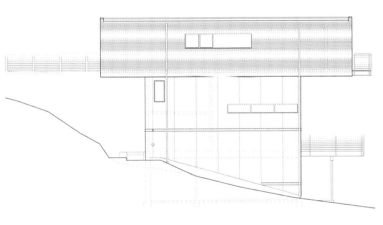

EAST ELEVATION

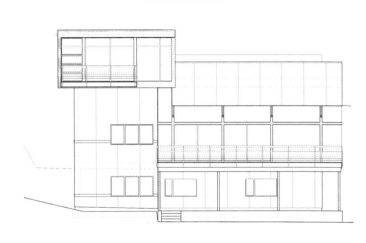

SOUTH ELEVATION

WEST ELEVATION

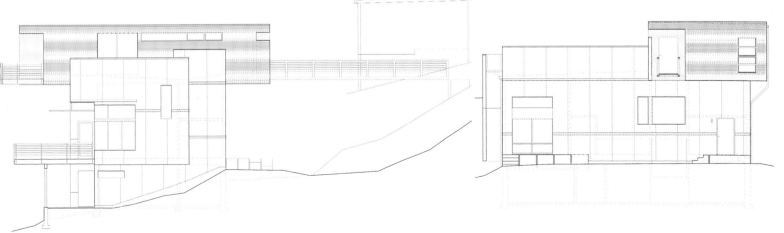

Entry to the house is via a steel bridge that leads to the upper
level, which is sheathed in low-maintenance Galvalume. The
entry leads to a two-story living room with aluminum-framed
windows that wrap around the space and provide panoramic
views of Puget Sound.

The loftlike second floor contains the dining, kitchen, and living areas, which open onto a deck with views of Puget Sound. Maple flooring and cabinets, along with the open metal staircase and aluminum-framed windows, give the space a crisp, contemporary look.

A soaring cypress canopy marks the west entrance to this property. A narrow band of clerestory windows brings south light to the interior.

TEXAS TWISTER

FOR THE BIRDS

The owners of this ranch, forty-five minutes south of Dallas, are avid bird-watchers who are reintroducing wetlands, native grasses, and indigenous bird populations to the property. The house is oriented on an east-west axis between hardwoods and an open meadow. The west entrance is situated between the woods and a smaller stand of live oak that shades the entry and west carport from the afternoon sun. A steeply angled cypress screen announces the entrance to the home for arriving guests.

The structure's roofs are supported by a twelve-foot on-center post-and-beam system that allows the roof to float above the main body of the building. A two-foot band of clerestory windows extends around the main house and guest quarters and provides an abundance of natural light. Along the cooler north side of the main residence, a wall of windows parallels an eight-foot-wide sitting porch and runs most of the length of the building. A wooden bridge connects this sitting porch to the two-bedroom guest quarters and a large outdoor dining porch with a fireplace. A water trough and birdbath extend east from the porch into the land-scape.

ARCHITECT
buildingstudio
PHOTOGRAPHER
Timothy Hursley

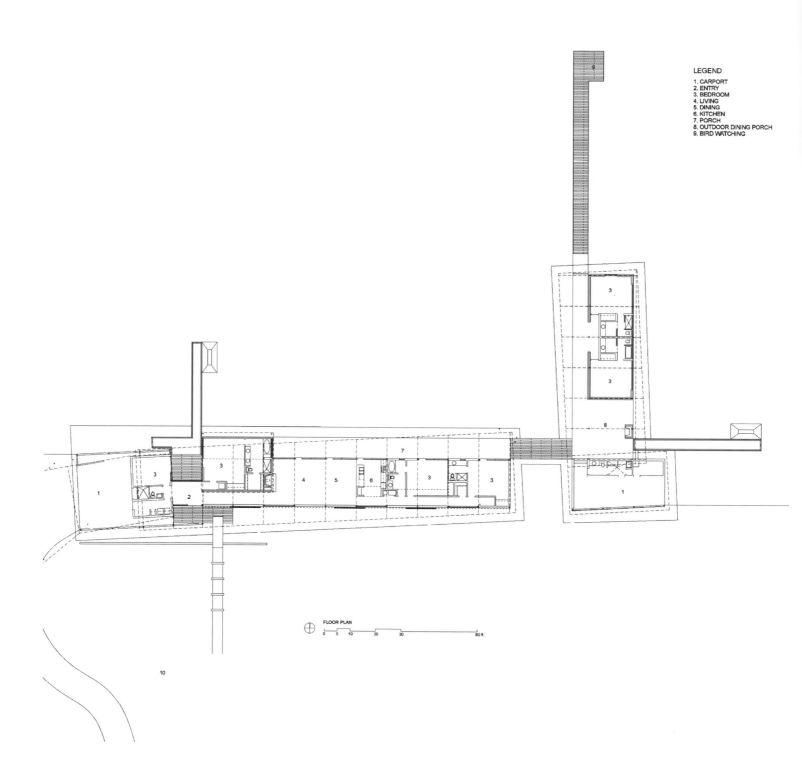

LEGEND

1. CARPORT
2. ENTRY
3. BEDROOM
4. LIVING
5. DINING
6. KITCHEN
7. PORCH
8. OUTDOOR DINING PORCH
9. BIRD WATCHING

FLOOR PLAN

0 5 10   20   30   60 ft.

A water trough and birdbath extend from the outdoor dining
porch into the landscape. The two-bedroom guest quarters
are to the right of the trough.

*The post-and-beam construction permits a continuous band
of clerestory windows along the perimeter of the house. A
wall of glass brings north light into the main living spaces.*

The massive roof floats above the guest quarters and outdoor
dining porch, sheltering them from the hot Texas sun.

*Inside the guest quarters, abundant natural light is provided
by the clerestory windows. At night, the wall of windows along
the north side frames the interior of the house. The windows
are equipped with metal pull-down doors for privacy.*

ASPEN HOUSE

VIEWS FROM EVERY CORNER

Built on a one-eighth-acre site in downtown Aspen, Colorado, this house has a modernist design that is in sharp contrast to the many themed architectural styles currently popular in the area. Rustic logs and stone, adobe, and Swiss chalet imitations are far more typical. And yet it fits comfortably within a community that has a rich architectural heritage, from early Victorian buildings to the Bauhaus sensibility of the nearby Aspen Institute.

The Aspen House is essentially a cube with an inverted residential plan, with the living, dining, and kitchen areas located on the second floor of the house, to take advantage of spectacular views of the mountains from every angle, while lifting the living areas above street level for privacy. Because the corners of the cube are glass, the diagonal views cut across the town grid so that mountain views are not blocked by the houses across the street.

The cube design accommodates five bedrooms, a separate caretaker's apartment on the lower level, and generous entertainment spaces on the the second level. One-third of the square footage of the house is below grade to reduce the impact of the house on the street. A central skylight brings light through a glass stairway to this lower level.

ARCHITECT
Peter L. Gluck and Partners, Architects
PHOTOGRAPHER
Paul Warchol

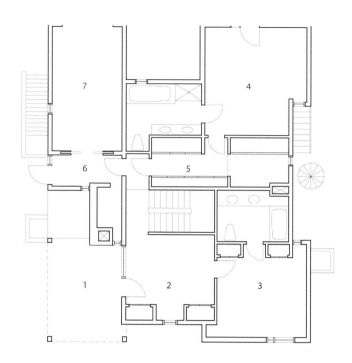

1	Living
2	Dining
3	Kitchen
4	Sitting area
5	Study
6	Terrace

1	Entry porch
2	Entry hall
3	Guest
4	Master bedroom
5	Dressing
6	Mudroom
7	Garage

SECTION   ELEVATION

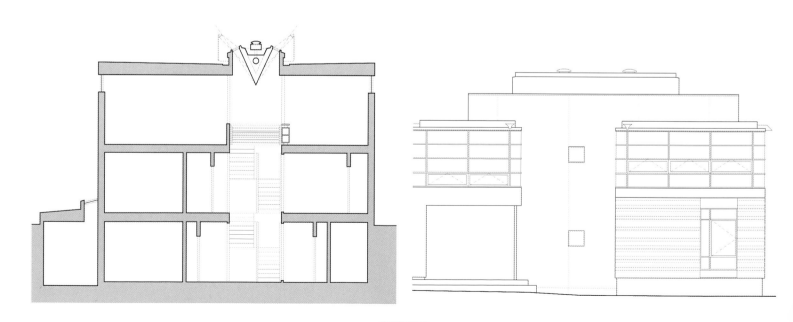

Previous pages and above: Large expanses of glass that wrap the corners on the second level provide unimpeded views of the mountains surrounding this resort community.

Located near the center of the cube, a large skylight in the glass stairway brings natural light deep into the house, which is partially submerged to comply with neighborhood height restrictions.

On the second level, the large central skylight and walls of corner-turning glass provide ample light and views for the open living, dining, and kitchen areas.

*Each area of the upstairs has its own corner-window configu-
ration, from the kitchen to the study to the large living area.*

The study enjoys an interesting architectural feature of an adjoining house without sacrificing distant views.

*The green-tinted glass facade of this house blends into the
landscape during the day. At night it is a glowing ribbon
across the steep site.*

CLIFFSIDE HOUSE

EMBRACING THE VIEW

The biggest challenge when designing this house was to maximize the exceptional views of the site while maintaining privacy and blending the sizable, 8,000-square-foot structure into the landscape. Located in Ecuador, this parcel faces part of the Andes Mountains, including Cotopaxi, the country's tallest snow-covered and still-active volcano.

The result is a house that embraces the clifflike nature of the site. The two main wings of the house extend in a wide angle to embrace the view and reach toward it. The east wing culminates in a cantilevered terrace that extends from the dining room on axis with Cotopaxi. From behind the west wing emerges a daring walkway that runs alongside a lap pool that is cantilevered high off a cliff. The walkway continues beyond the pool and offers panoramic views. The lap pool begins within the house and continues to the exterior.

The facade facing the mountains is almost entirely green-tinted glass, providing each room with uninterrupted views and also allowing the house to disappear into the landscape when viewed from across the valley. The facade facing the street is mostly solid, offering privacy for the family.

The dramatic interior consists of curving and sloping planes of glass, concrete, and maple that define living areas and frame the views.

ARCHITECT
Carlos Zapata Studio
PHOTOGRAPHER
Undine Prölh

SECOND-FLOOR PLAN

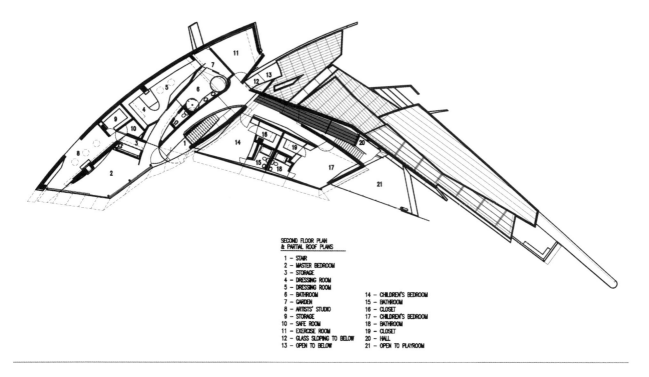

SECOND FLOOR PLAN
& PARTIAL ROOF PLANS

1 – STAIR
2 – MASTER BEDROOM
3 – STORAGE
4 – DRESSING ROOM
5 – DRESSING ROOM
6 – BATHROOM
7 – GARDEN
8 – ARTISTS' STUDIO
9 – STORAGE
10 – SAFE ROOM
11 – EXERCISE ROOM
12 – GLASS SLOPING TO BELOW
13 – OPEN TO BELOW
14 – CHILDREN'S BEDROOM
15 – BATHROOM
16 – CLOSET
17 – CHILDREN'S BEDROOM
18 – BATHROOM
19 – CLOSET
20 – HALL
21 – OPEN TO PLAYROOM

FIRST-FLOOR PLAN

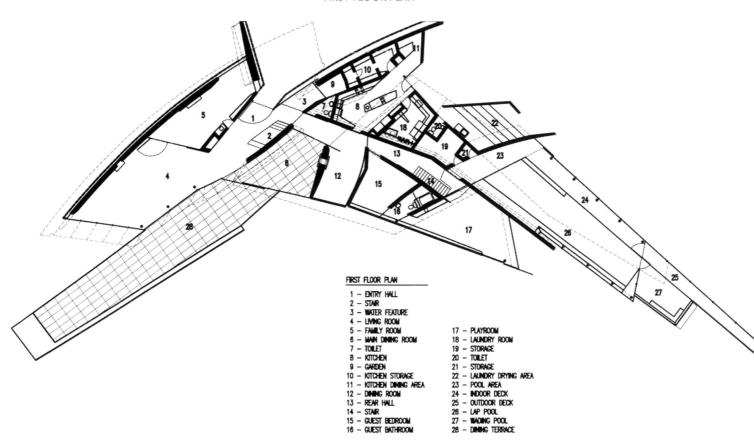

FIRST FLOOR PLAN

1 – ENTRY HALL
2 – STAIR
3 – WATER FEATURE
4 – LIVING ROOM
5 – FAMILY ROOM
6 – MAIN DINING ROOM
7 – TOILET
8 – KITCHEN
9 – GARDEN
10 – KITCHEN STORAGE
11 – KITCHEN DINING AREA
12 – DINING ROOM
13 – REAR HALL
14 – STAIR
15 – GUEST BEDROOM
16 – GUEST BATHROOM
17 – PLAYROOM
18 – LAUNDRY ROOM
19 – STORAGE
20 – TOILET
21 – STORAGE
22 – LAUNDRY DRYING AREA
23 – POOL AREA
24 – INDOOR DECK
25 – OUTDOOR DECK
26 – LAP POOL
27 – WADING POOL
28 – DINING TERRACE

SOUTHWEST ELEVATION

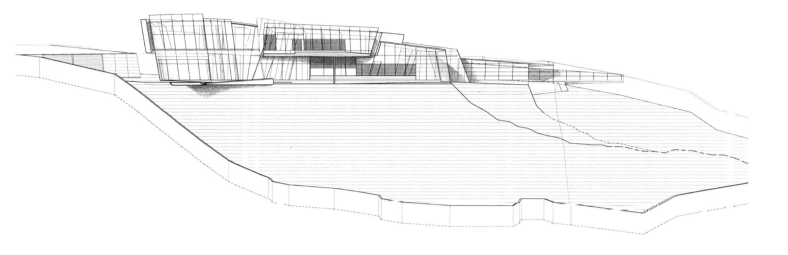

NORTHWEST ELEVATION

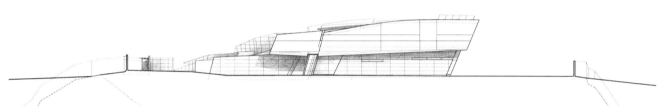

NORTHEAST ELEVATION

SITE PLAN

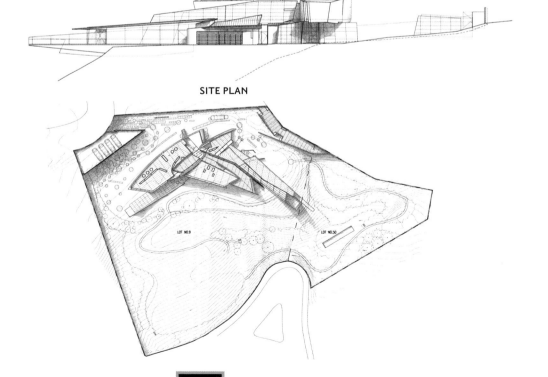

The terrace extends from the dining room, passes the living room, and terminates at a water feature. Above the living room is the master bedroom suite. The lap pool opposite begins inside the house and terminates outside at a wading pool.

Inside the house is a maze of complex forms. At the left is a view of the entry and dining area and above is the living area. The glass facade bends forward, embracing the landscape. Dramatic glass walls contrast with dense interior walls of poured-in-place concrete.

*At the entry, the staircase soars to the second floor like a piece
of abstract sculpture. At the second-floor landing, its curved
glass acts as the guardrail.*

72

NGH

*The massive glass walls continue to the second-floor master
bedroom, which has direct views of the volcano.*

PACKARD KOMORIYA RESIDENCE

GLASS BRIDGES IN THE FOREST

This house is clad in cedar shingles and accentuated with board-formed concrete and dry-stacked stone to give it the appearance, from the exterior at least, of a structure firmly rooted in the ground. Once inside, and particularly from the second-floor public areas, this impression quickly changes. Beginning at the entry, an approximately seventy-foot-long wall of glass draws the eye past the kitchen, dining area, and living room out to the trees as it wraps around the end of the living room. The effect is one of floating above the landscape rather than being attached to it. Three shed-roofed buildings that are connected by a series of long, flat-roofed, glass-walled "bridges" are positioned to intimately engage this 4,200-square-foot dwelling with the surrounding wooded landscape. The ceiling in the dining area and living room follows the contour of the shed roof, beginning low at the entry and soaring to double height at the end where the glass wall makes it turn. A second shed contains the master bedroom suite. Below these sheds are guest bedrooms and storage. A third shed contains the garage.

The interior materials and finishes are spare and are derived from natural materials that include bluestone flooring in the entry area, Brazilian cherry flooring, and maple cabinetry and shelving throughout the house.

ARCHITECT
Robert M. Gurney Architect
PHOTOGRAPHER
Hoachlander-Davis Photography

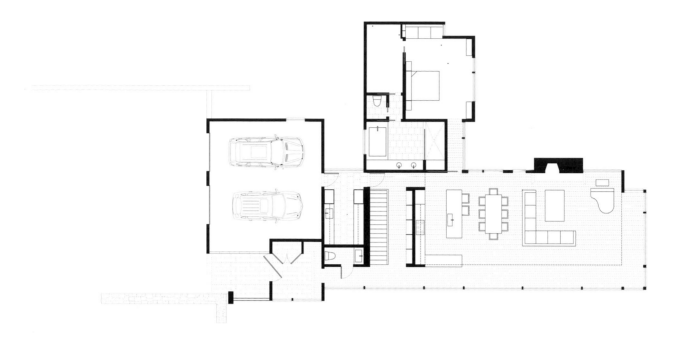

LOWER-LEVEL PLAN

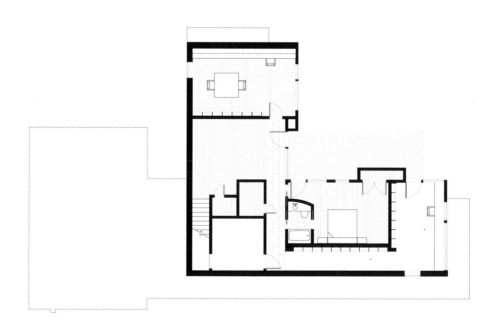

EAST ELEVATION   NORTH ELEVATION

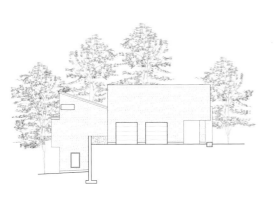 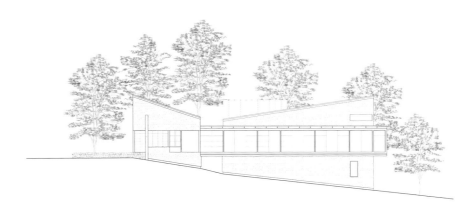

WEST ELEVATION   SOUTH ELEVATION

 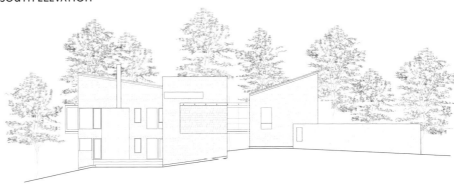

*Previous pages and above: The house, on a five-acre wooded
lot in Potomac, Maryland, is designed and sited to take
advantage of the sloping topography and views of the surrounding forest.*

Warm woods and dry-stacked stone welcome visitors at the entry. A wall of glass parallels the principal living areas of the house, drawing attention to the surrounding forest.

A view of the entry from the living area. Just past the entry, a staircase descends to the guest bedrooms.

*The ceiling gradually rises to double height at the end of the
living area. The open kitchen, dining, and living room forms
a large, informal entertaining area surrounded by nature.
On the following pages, this part of the house appears to be
thrust out into nature.*

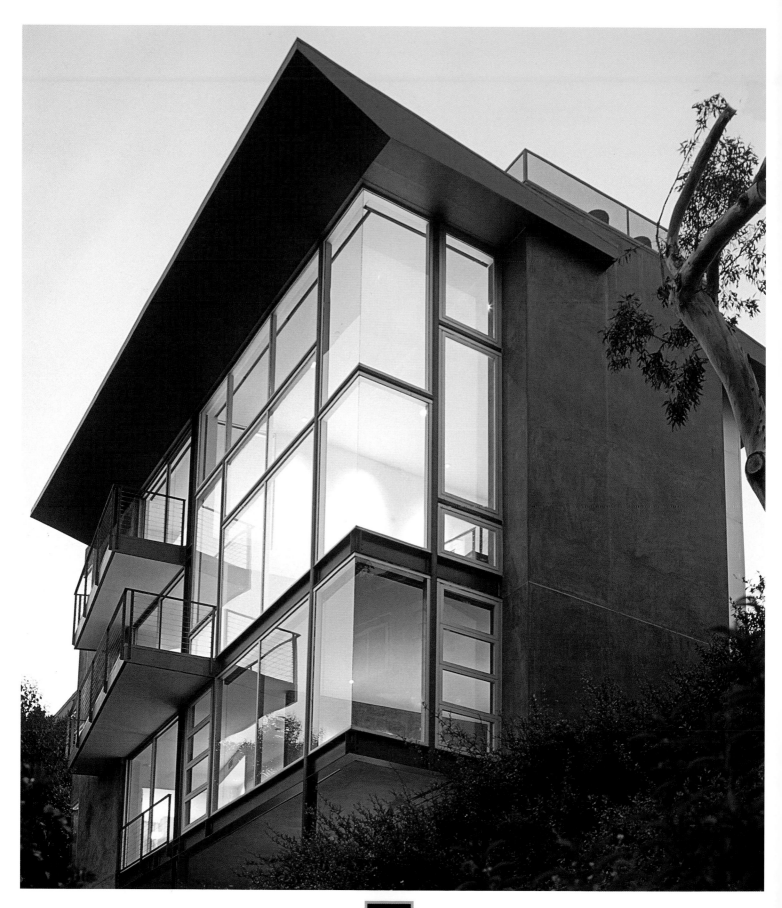

LEONARD RESIDENCE

LIFE IN THE HILLS

This 4,000-square-foot residence is situated on a 45-degree downward slope of a canyon in the Hollywood Hills of Los Angeles. Embracing an entry courtyard, the structure is a composition of vast areas of glass supported by steel and concrete. The design of the house recalls the midcentury case-study houses by Richard Neutra in Southern California. With multiple levels, the house descends the slope. Each level caters to the specific living, working, and relaxation needs of its owners. The glass walls are carefully positioned to frame classic L.A. views while shielding the interior of the house from adjacent homes in this dense urban location.

At the entrance level, a permanently installed corten steel and glass dining table, designed by the architect, greets the visitor. A two-story living room is suspended over the canyon on a concrete slab that also serves as the finished floor. Above, the master bedroom suite with a reading loft has panoramic views through twenty-foot-high glass walls. A private roof deck is strategically positioned above the garage and shielded from view.

From the main public level, a staircase anchored to a cast-in-place concrete wall descends to the lower level, which contains a home office, guest quarters, and storage.

ARCHITECT
Steven Ehrlich Architects
PHOTOGRAPHER
Grey Crawford

MAIN LEVEL   UPPER LEVEL   WEST ELEVATION

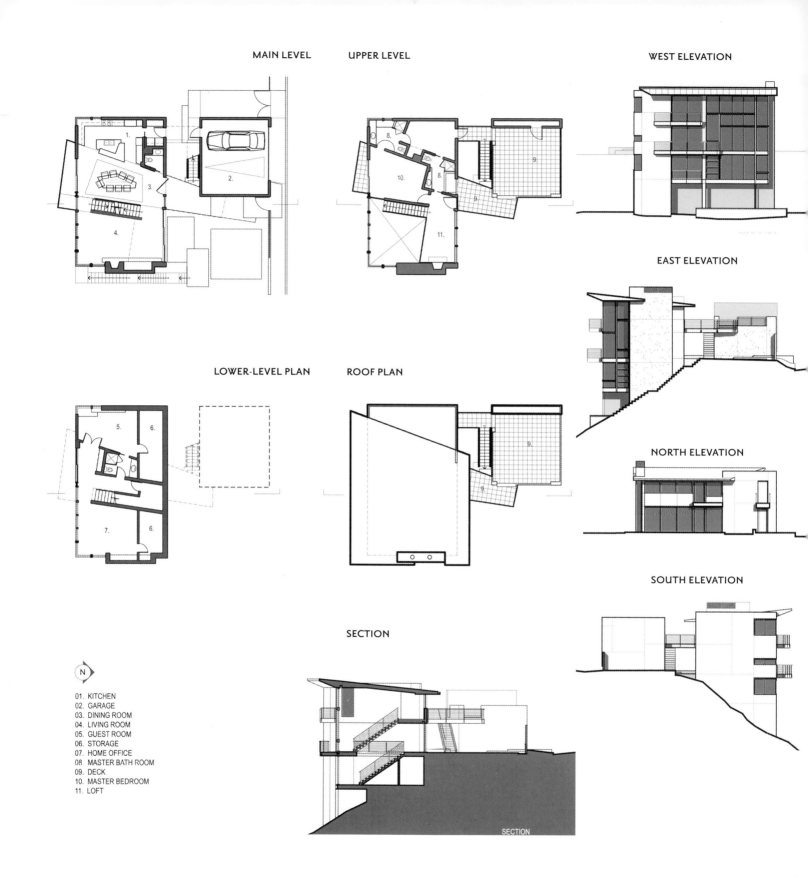

LOWER-LEVEL PLAN   ROOF PLAN

                                                          EAST ELEVATION

                                                          NORTH ELEVATION

              SECTION

                                                          SOUTH ELEVATION

N

01. KITCHEN
02. GARAGE
03. DINING ROOM
04. LIVING ROOM
05. GUEST ROOM
06. STORAGE
07. HOME OFFICE
08. MASTER BATH ROOM
09. DECK
10. MASTER BEDROOM
11. LOFT

Previous pages and above: The house is spliced into multiple levels to accommodate and embrace the steep slope yet make the most of all usable space and the panoramic views while providing privacy from the adjacent homes.

*The entry to the main level enjoys a view through the living
room to the city beyond. There is a terrace above the garage,
and another terrace extends off the master bedroom.*

The two-story living room appears to be suspended over the
canyon. An open staircase leads to the master suite.

Upon entering the house, the visitor is greeted by the permanently installed corten steel and glass dining table designed by
the architect. Opposite, glass wraps around the corner of the
vanity in the master bedroom, providing panoramic views
from the glass-enclosed shower. On the following pages,
extensive glazing reveals the L.A. sprawl below.

Large, rectangular openings frame interior and exterior views of this Long Island home. All major rooms open onto a pool deck.

SAGAPONAC HOUSE

MODERN SIMPLICITY

This 4,600-square-foot home is sited on just under three acres of wooded land between the fashionable South and East Hampton areas of Long Island, New York. In contrast to most of the oversized and opulent country houses in this summer playground, this weekend retreat is decidedly modern and understated. Sitting low and tight to the flat landscape, it is composed of two simple rectangular volumes forming an L-shaped plan. These volumes wrap around and embrace the main public space, which is a swimming pool, multilevel terraces, and a covered porch with a shower. This space is accessible and visible from every room in the house and acts as a stage for daily activities. The dramatic and deep-set placement of the aluminum-and-glass sliding panels within these volumes engages and frames these exterior spaces as well as the natural landscape. Conversely, when outside, these same openings serve to frame the interior spaces of the house.

The house is sheathed in horizontally laid western red cedar that will turn a soft silvery gray as it ages. Exterior detailing is simple and precise, with stucco and clear anodized-aluminum paneling used for accents. Turkish travertine is used for the pool area.

ARCHITECT
Hariri & Hariri
PHOTOGRAPHER
Paul Warchol

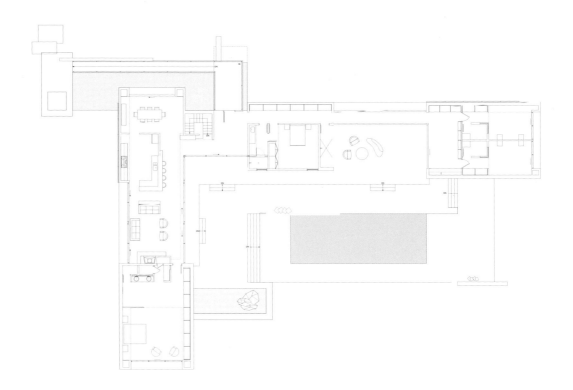

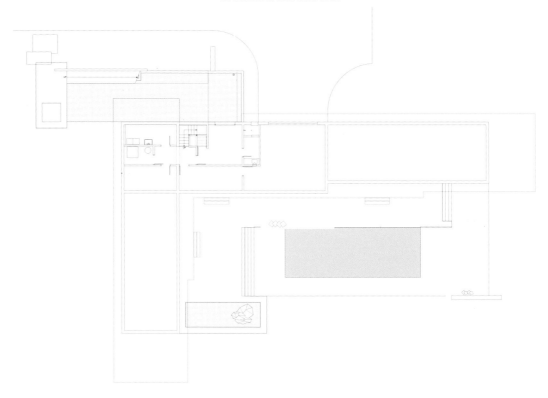

ELEVATION

WEST ELEVATION

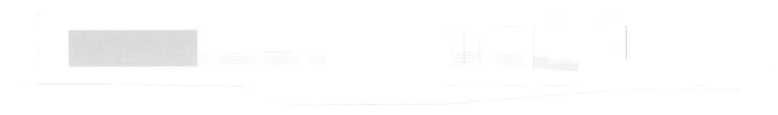

SECTION

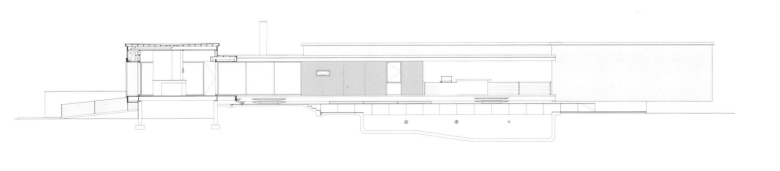

A concrete ramp leads to the entry, marked by a concrete monolith. The large, deep-set aluminum-framed windows provide views of the interior of the house.

A lanai overlooks the pool and is open on both sides for cross
breezes. It can also be completely enclosed in inclement
weather.

The dining area and kitchen as seen from the entry ramp.

The floors are Brazilian walnut. This wing of the house contains the kitchen and dining areas, the living area, and the master suite.

The master bedroom and bathroom with walls, shower, and tiles made of glass. The following pages show the guest bedrooms and lanai in the wing to the right, with the living area directly ahead. The broad, horizontal bands of glass frame and define the living spaces.

EAST SIDE TOWN HOUSE

UPDATED MODERN

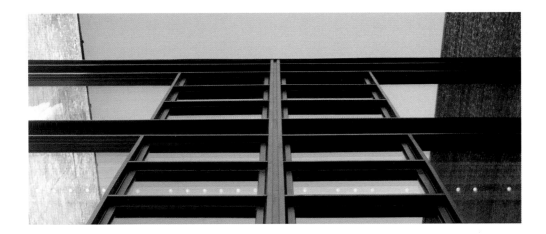

This project consisted of the renovation and expansion of a 1958 glass town house on New York's Upper East Side. A third floor was added, extending the glass facade vertically while respecting the vocabulary of the original design. The interior was gutted except for the main floor, where original finishes were maintained. Here, loftlike space for living, dining, and kitchen open to the exterior with large glass walls on either side.

A new staircase within a light-filled atrium leads to the upper levels. The second level has two children's bedrooms, with a master bedroom in the front. The master bath, with walls and floors of white statuary slab marble and glass, is open to the bedroom. The third-level landing has glass-block floors that allow light from the skylight above to flow into the center of the house. A sophisticated media room is located on this level. It is acoustically isolated and open on one side to a terrace and on the other to the atrium. The room is framed by pear-wood cabinets, which hold the owners' extensive collection of CDs within a double-layered system of shelves and doors. On this upper level there is also a guest room and an office. On the half level below the street is the playfully colored children's playroom and exercise area.

ARCHITECT
Alexander Gorlin Architects
PHOTOGRAPHER
Peter Aaron, ESTO

THIRD-FLOOR PLAN   SECOND-FLOOR PLAN   FIRST-FLOOR PLAN   BASEMENT PLAN   NORTH ELEVATION

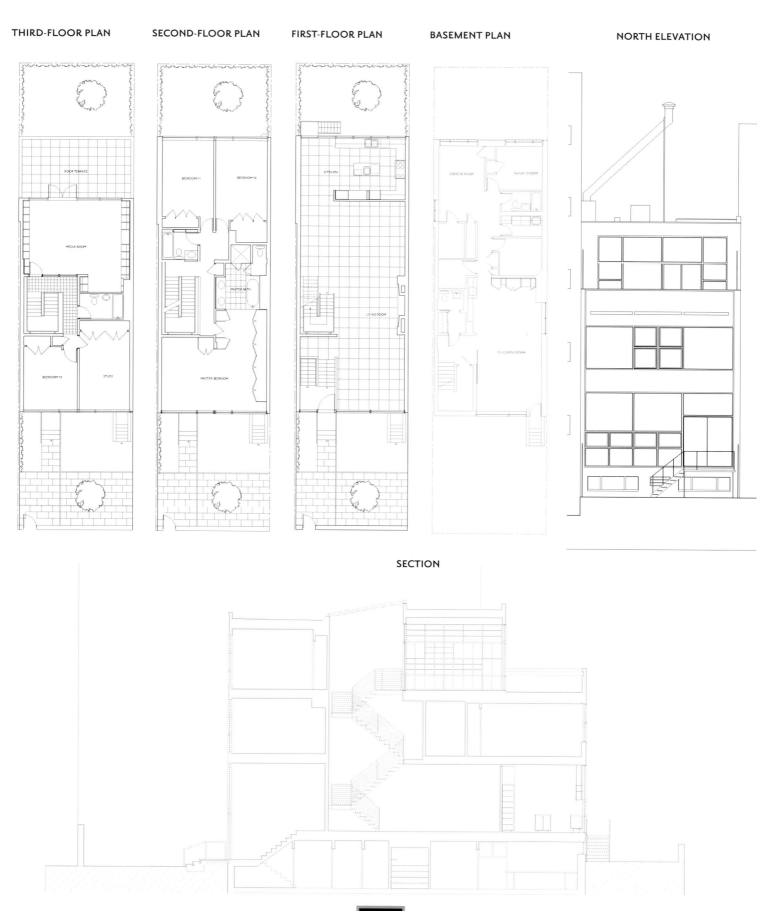

SECTION

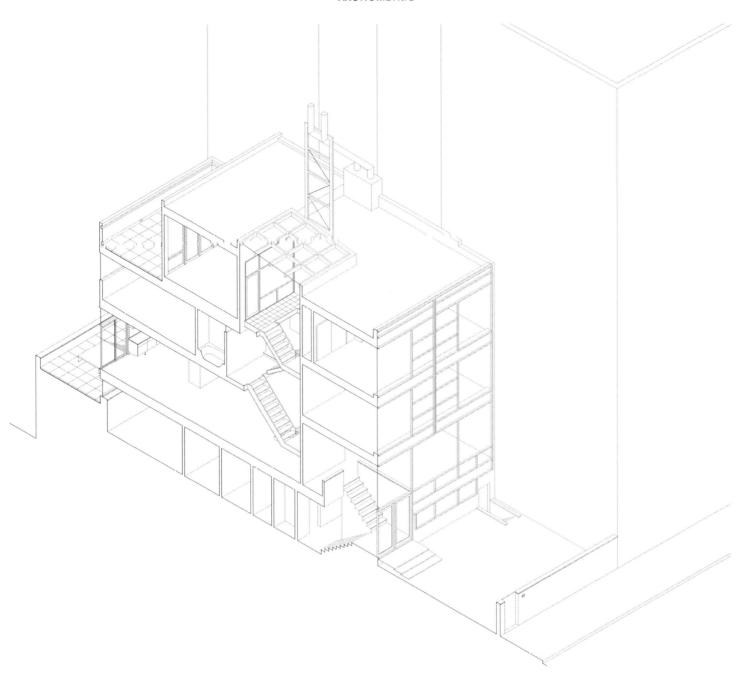

*On the previous pages: The vertical glass facade gives the
town house a strong presence on the street, even though it is
set back twenty-five feet from the sidewalk.*

A red door greets visitors from the street. At the rear, the house steps back to allow for a terrace for the media room on the third floor.

A view from the dining room past the living area to the street.
The staircase is lit by natural light as it ascends to the atrium.

The living area opens onto the dining area, with the kitchen beyond.

The glass wall of the kitchen provides natural light for the
translucent cabinets mounted in front of it.

*The master bathroom, which opens onto the master bed-
room, is paneled in white slab marble. The cabinetry
throughout the master suite is warm pear wood.*

The third-floor landing is glass block, allowing light to penetrate from the skylight above into the lower reaches of the house. At the third level, an extremely clear, low-iron-content glass wall separates the media room from the landing.

The media room is framed by pear-wood cabinets, which hold the owners' extensive collection of CDs within a double-layered system of shelves and doors. The media room is seen here from the landing (left) and from the terrace (above).

Appearing as a beacon for scholarship, this modest structure
presents an elegant solution for study and document storage.

SCHOLAR'S LIBRARY

A LOOKOUT FOR LEARNING

This private library is located on a family retreat in New York's Catskill Mountains. Also on the property is a restored 150-year-old farmhouse and a recently constructed guest dormitory that sleeps up to twenty-five family members and friends. The library contains an all-glass study space above, and below is storage for approximately ten thousand books for a scholar of Japanese history.

Built on a tight budget, the library is a cube, measuring approximately twenty feet in dimension. The lower exterior is sheathed in inexpensive concrete board. The upper study floor contains linear workspace with continuous glass on all four sides. The large glass panels on the southeast and northwest corners open for cross ventilation. Below, in the windowless storage space, the tightly packed stacks are designed to preserve the books and minimize the cost of heating during the winter months.

The changing weather, seasons, and time of day unfold for anyone sitting in this high perch located just on the edge of the woods. While completely private, the building also serves as a lookout post for the surrounding property.

ARCHITECT
Peter L. Gluck and Partners, Architects
PHOTOGRAPHER
Paul Warchol

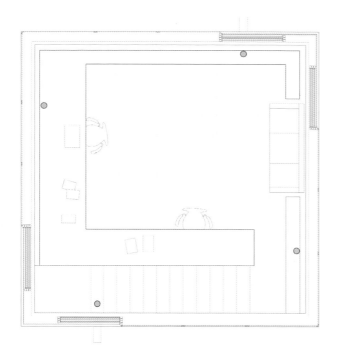

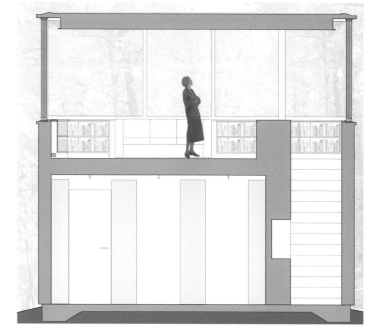

SITE PLAN

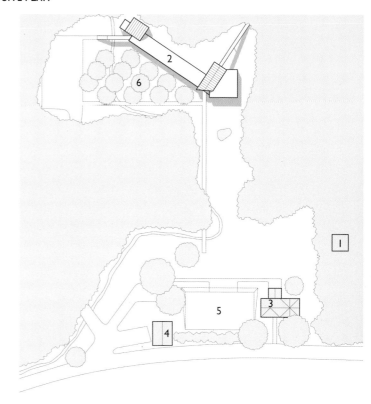

LOWER-FLOOR PLAN

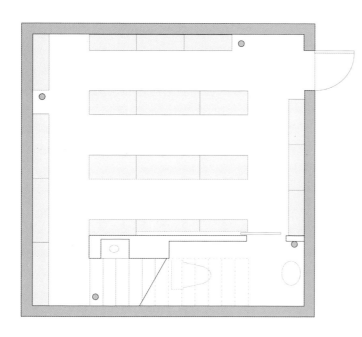

1 Library
2 Guest dormitory
3 Farmhouse
4 Barn
5 Badminton court
6 Orchard

*The unfinished concrete board forming the base of the library
is well suited to the rock outcropping surrounding it.*

In the study, the worktops are concrete and have ample storage for books beneath. Steel supports allow the roof to seemingly float above the study, which is also equipped with a sofa for relaxing.

*Beneath the study, approximately ten thousand books are
stored in standard steel bookcases.*

The ground-level entry stair of this coastal Florida home is encased in a glass box. The first-floor blue-glazed windows running the length of the house on both sides make it a transparent box. The roof of the second floor is raised. The master suite and guest bedrooms have broad terraces and panoramic views.

GULF COAST RESIDENCE

AN ATRIUM UNITES IT

This modern glass dwelling is a long, rectangular structure elevated on pilings to lift it above storm floods and to capture water views from both sides on this narrow strip of land between the Gulf of Mexico and Little Sarasota Bay in Florida.

The entrance stair on the ground level is located beneath a central atrium. A glass floor above brings natural light down to this level from the generous skylight covering the atrium. A dichroic glass prism in the atrium diffuses daylight from clerestory windows into a spectrum of colors that shift with the viewing angle to reflect subtle nuances in the center of the house during the day. At night the prism is illuminated by fiber optics.

Specially coated plate-glass windows cast a cool, blue light on the interiors, while upper panes of translucent and patterned glass control heat gain. The concrete-block walls are designed to provide a thermal mass, absorbing heat during the day and reradiating it at night when it is cool. Large overhangs and multiple windows further conserve energy by allowing the house to be naturally ventilated.

The public areas of the house on the first floor flow from the atrium. The master bedroom and guest bedrooms are grouped around the atrium on the second level.

ARCHITECT
Toshiko Mori Architect
PHOTOGRAPHER
Paul Warchol

SECOND-FLOOR PLAN

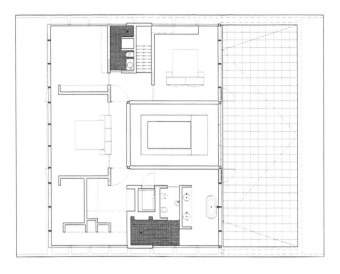

FIRST-FLOOR PLAN

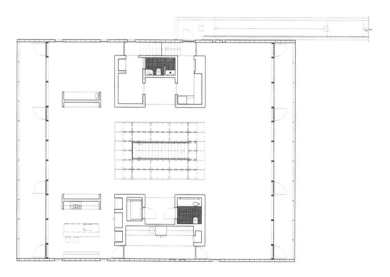

FOUNDATION PLAN

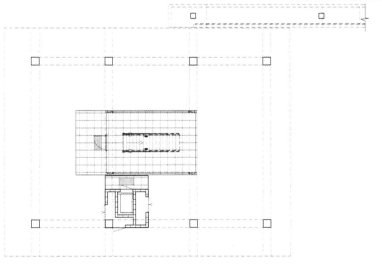

A view of the terrace outside the second-floor master suite and bathroom.

ELEVATION

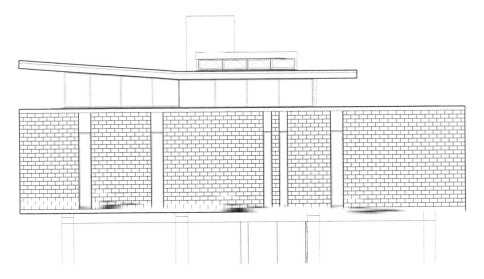

ELEVATION

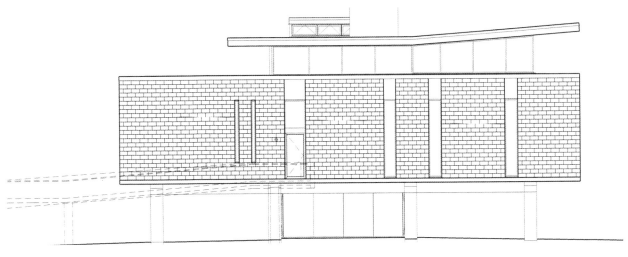

SECTION

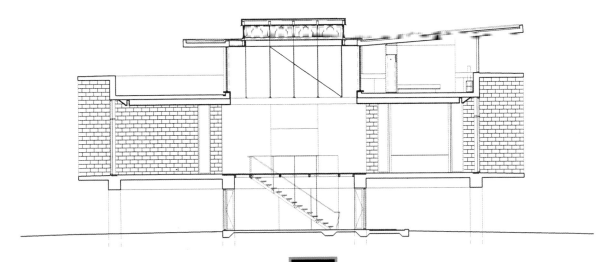

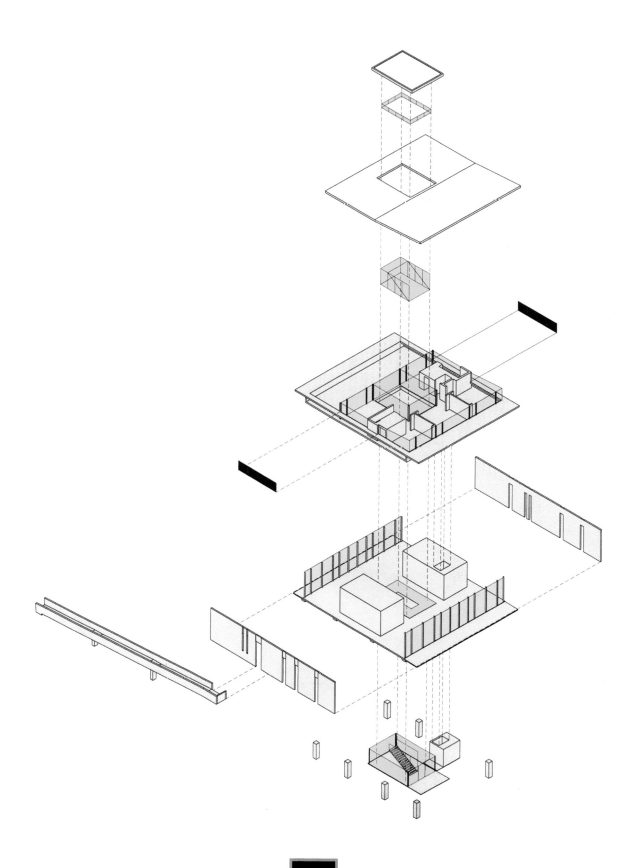

The house may also be accessed via a gently sloping entry
bridge that leads directly to the first-floor living area.

Wide steps lead from the ground level to the first floor. Glass
flooring surrounding the stairs brings light from the large,
dramatic central atrium. A glass prism within the atrium diffuses daylight into a spectrum of colors.

Grouped around the atrium, the living and dining areas enjoy diffused natural light from the large clerestory windows and the walls of glazing on either end of this level.

The special blue coating on the windows is evident in the
minimalist stainless-steel kitchen.

The master bath opens onto a large second-floor terrace,
while the ribbon windows in the master bedroom offer
panoramic water views. Fiber-optic light animates the atrium
at night, from the ground level to the second floor.

This guest house is sited on a plateau overlooking a California vineyard. The east facade is a wall of glazing and the west facade is a thick wall of native earth.

VINEYARD RESIDENCE

RAMMED EARTH AND GLASS

This three-bedroom guest house is nestled between a vineyard and a forest at the foot of Sonoma Mountain in California. A heavy rammed-earth wall demarcates the primary spaces of the house. Built of native dirt, this massive earthen wall anchors the building structurally, ecologically, and experientially. Parallel floor and ceiling planes extend to the east, where floor-to-ceiling glass allows sweeping views over the vineyard, valley, and distant hills.

Carefully placed among existing trees, the house is oriented to provide natural heating and cooling. Floor-to-ceiling east-facing glass gathers warmth from the morning sun, tempered during summer months by deep roof overhangs. The solid west wall and wooded hillside shade the house from intense afternoon heat. A clerestory cut into the roof brings sun and sky deep into the interior and ventilates the house with natural convection currents.

ARCHITECT
Aidlin Darling Design
PHOTOGRAPHERS
John Sutton, J. D. Peterson

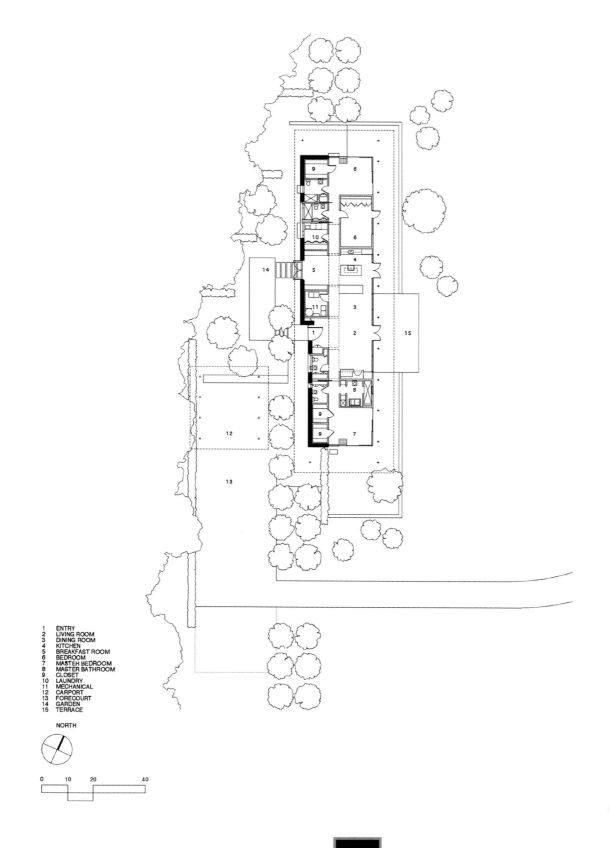

1 ENTRY
2 LIVING ROOM
3 DINING ROOM
4 KITCHEN
5 BREAKFAST ROOM
6 BEDROOM
7 MASTER BEDROOM
8 MASTER BATHROOM
9 CLOSET
10 LAUNDRY
11 MECHANICAL
12 CARPORT
13 FORECOURT
14 GARDEN
15 TERRACE

NORTH

0   10   20   40

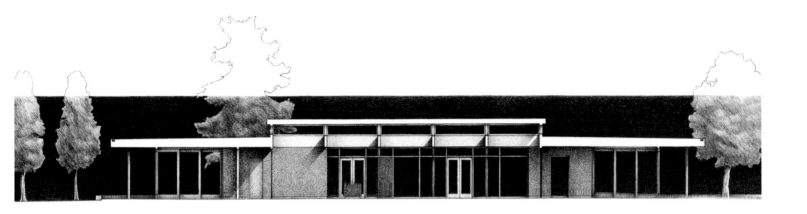

ELEVATION   ELEVATION

*Entry is through the massive rammed-earth wall that anchors
the structure. Corner sliding glass doors open the interior to
the surrounding terraces, embracing the indoor-outdoor
lifestyle made possible by Sonoma's temperate climate.*

The dwelling's rich materials palette of earth, concrete, wood, plaster, and steel is balanced by a simplicity of form and detail.

*The kitchen opens to a view of the vineyard. The breakfast
room overlooks a tranquil garden setting.*

*The careful detailing evident throughout the house extends to
the bathroom vanities. Floor-to-ceiling corner sliding doors
in the master bedroom open to create the sense of an outdoor
room.*

*The glass-walled living area of this urban California home
overlooks a reflecting pool. A high wall surrounds this first-
floor level, providing privacy and acting as a noise barrier for
this busy downtown corner location.*

THE PROSPECT

HORIZONTAL PANES

This highly innovative home in downtown La Jolla, California, is located on a 7,200-square-foot lot that formerly held a service station—an abandoned brownfield site, vacant since 1992. The architect-owner used the space to build a private, sustainable, urban residence and architectural studio. The residence is a stucco box resting on and supported by corten steel wall planes, providing both privacy and noise attenuation on this busy corner location. Walls of glass open the main living area to a reflecting pool on one side and a glass floor on the other. This floor becomes the ceiling of the studio and recreation facilities below, transforming this below-grade space into a brightly lit yet private retreat.

Upstairs are guest bedrooms and the master suite, which has glass walls and a generous balcony that opens to magnificent views in this seaside community.

ARCHITECT
Jonathan Segal
PHOTOGRAPHER
David Hewitt / Anne Garrison, Jimmy Fluker
Paul Brody, Steve Simpson, Jonathan Segal

GROUND-FLOOR PLAN

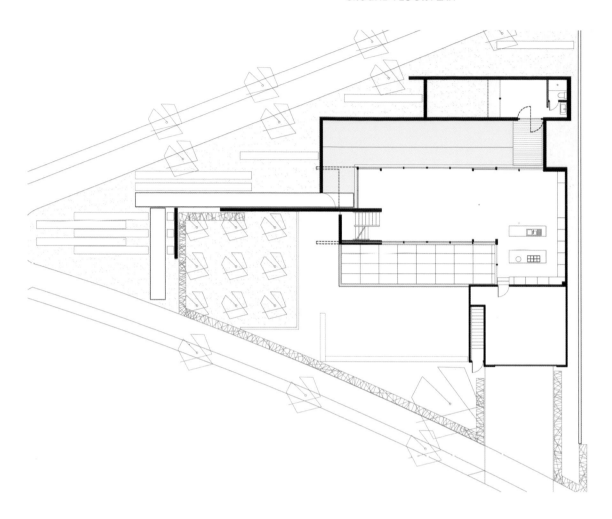

NORTH ELEVATION

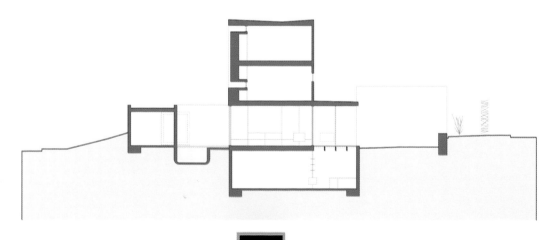

Extensive soil remediation was required turn this former gas station site into a lush, plant-rich garden.

Mimicking the reflecting pool on the opposite side of the living area, a glass floor brings natural light into the architect's studio below ground level.

The kitchen and dining areas are located on the main level,
with a small, glass-enclosed study beyond. The master bed-
room is visible from the master bathroom with
glass-enclosed shower.

The master bedroom opens onto a large terrace with views across La Jolla. The main living area is seen from across the glass ceiling of the studio.

Architects

Chicago Town House

www.gorlinarchitects.com
Alexander Gorlin Architects
137 Varick Street
New York, NY 10013
212-229-1199

Shelving Rock Residence

www.bcj.com
Bohlin Cywinski Jackson
123 Broad Street, Suite 1370
Philadelphia, PA 19109
215-790-5900

Milepost 9

www.cobbarch.com
E. Cobb Architects
911 Western Avenue #318
Seattle, WA 98104
206-287-0136

Texas Twister

www.buildingstudio.com
buildingstudio
431 South Main Street, Second Floor
Memphis, TN 38103
901-527-3086

Aspen House

www.gluckpartners.com
Peter L. Gluck and Partners, Architects
646 West 131st Street
New York, NY 10027
212-690-4950

Cliffside House
www.wood-zapata.com
Carlos Zapata Studio
100 South Street
Boston, MA 02111
617-728-3636

Packard Komoriya Residence
www.robertgurneyarchitect.com
Robert M. Gurney Architect
113 South Patrick Street
Alexandria, VA 22314
703-739-3843

Leonard Residence
www.s-ehrlich.com
Stephen Ehrlich Architects
10865 Washington Boulevard
Culver City, CA
310-838-9700

Sagaponac House
www.haririandhariri.com
Hariri & Hariri
18 East 12th Street
New York, NY 10003
212-727-0338

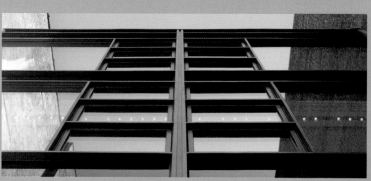

East Side Town House
www.gorlinarchitects.com
Alexander Gorlin Architects
137 Varick Street
New York, NY 10013
212-229-1199

Scholar's Library

www.gluckpartners.com

Peter L. Gluck and Partners, Architects
646 West 131st Street
New York, NY 10027
212-690-4950

Gulf Coast Residence

www.tmarch.com

Toshiko Mori Architect
180 Varick Street, Suite 1322
New York, NY 10014
212-337-9644

Vineyard Residence

www.aidlindarlingdesign.com

Aidlin Darling Design
500 Third Street, Suite 410
San Francisco, CA 94107
414-974-5603

The Prospect

www.jonathansegal.com

Jonathan Segal
1165 19th Street, Suite A
San Diego, CA 92101
619-255-1315